The Weather Person's Handbook

By: Christopher Nance

Illustrated By:
Khashayar and Ardavan Javid

First Edition

Printed in the United States of America
By: Peggy Anvari at
City Wide Printing, Van Nuys, CA

Published by
Christopher Productions, Inc.
CPI Publishers
10153 1/2 Riverside Drive #266
Toluca Lake, CA 91602
(818) 831-9268

ISBN 0-9648363-1-9
LIBRARY OF CONGRESS CATALOG CARD NUMBER : 97-094527

Acknowledgments

Special thanks to Tanny Wiggins for the Editing of this book.

Special thanks to Paul Villar, my Personal Assistant and Publisher, for all the hard work and long hours.

Special thanks to my darling Sam. My Editor, Publisher and best friend.

A Message From The Author...

This is a fun way to learn. This handbook not only allows the reader to be creative, it also encourages hands on learning through fun to do experiments that are safe. Read this book with a young person and let the learning begin.

• • • • •

While growing up and going to school, I had teachers that made learning fun and challenged my thinking. I had teachers that took a lot of the joy out of learning. This workbook is designed to show boys and girls how much fun science and math can really be.

We live in a world of science and numbers, and without knowing it we use them in everyday activities. When we walk or talk or bounce a ball, fly a kite or drive a car, it all involves science and math.

The more you learn, the more you'll be able to do. So have fun with this book and set your sights high.

Happy Weather,
Christopher Nance - Weatherdude

About the Illustrators...

Ardavan and Khashayar (K.J.) Javid are twin brothers who met Christopher Nance in 1994 while interning at NBC 4 in the field of meteorology.

While working there, Christopher discovered their artistic talents and put them in charge of illustrating his second children's book entitled "Before There Were People." Ever since, they have become Christopher Nance's exclusive artists, illustrating his third book, "The Weatherman is Coming to my School Today" and now, this workbook. At the age of 26, K.J. and Ardavan have recently graduated from California State University Northridge with a degree in meteorology and are now pursuing a career in graphic arts.

To all the boys and girls who like to make learning fun.
Set your goals high and make your dreams come true...

- The Weatherdude

Christopher Nance

Why I Became A Weather Forecaster.

When I was in elementary school, I was not the smartest kid in school. I liked science and I was lucky to have a few wonderful teachers who taught me that I didn't have to always get great grades to be a success, as long as I always did my best. So, no matter what class I took, I always tried my best. Sometimes I'd get an "A" or "B" and sometimes I just got a passing grade, but no matter what the grade, if it was my best work I felt proud.

One day my class went on a field trip to an airport. A sleek jet dropped out of the sky and landed near us. The pilot jumped out and told us all, how cool science was. We were all impressed as he climbed back in his jet and flew away; from that day, I knew I wanted to be involved with science.

When I was old enough to make my own decisions, I took as many science classes as I could and knew that no matter what I did for a living, it would involve science and math.

Each day I work as a weather forecaster in Southern California and help moms, dads, boys and girls decide how to dress for that day. Whether it's rainy, sunny or windy, I'm always happy because I'm doing what I like.

THE WEATHER EFFECTS EVERYTHING...

The weather effects everything, from the clothes you wear to the food you eat. Let's say you are getting ready for school and you want to dress for cold weather. You go to your room and select the following cotton clothes: your underwear, socks, shirt, jacket and gloves. If it were not for the cotton plant you would not have these clothes. Now what type of weather is needed to make the cotton plant grow? You need sun and rain to make it grow.

Now that you are dressed for cold weather, you want to eat a good breakfast to keep your body going. What type of food will you have for breakfast? You have orange juice, which comes from orange trees; you have toast, which comes from wheat, and hot oatmeal that comes from oats. Now if it were not for the sun and the rain to make theses plants grow, you would not have breakfast. Can you think of any other things that you would wear or eat that depend on the weather?

1 _____

2 _____

3 _____

4 _____

5 _____

6 _____

7 _____

¥ Did you know that the dinosaurs died off many years ago, because of big changes in the weather, especially a drop in the amount of sunlight?

WEATHER WORKS WONDERS!

ENERGY + RAIN + COTTON PLANTS = CLOTHES

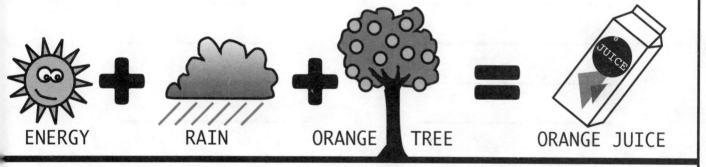

ENERGY + RAIN + ORANGE TREE = ORANGE JUICE

ENERGY + RAIN + WHEAT & OATS = BREAD & CEREAL

WHAT DID YOU EAT TODAY, AND DO YOU KNOW WHERE IT CAME FROM?

FOOD	SOURCE
_____	_____
_____	_____
_____	_____
_____	_____
_____	_____
_____	_____
_____	_____
_____	_____
_____	_____
_____	_____

WEATHER TERMS

To understand how the weather works, we need to know some of the tools and terms used by weather forecasters.

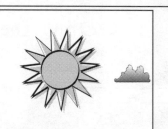

CLEAR
Little or no clouds in the sky.

SUNNY
The sun is out and the sky is bright.

HAZY
The sun is out, but because of smog, dust or fog, the sky is not as bright.

PARTLY CLOUDY
There are some clouds in the sky.

OVERCAST
A thin layer of clouds in the sky that allows enough sunlight so you can still see your shadow.

CLOUDY
Most of the sky is covered with clouds.

FOG
A cloud that forms at the surface of the Earth.

DRIZZLE
Tiny droplets of water that fall or float slowly to the ground.

RAIN
Water drops falling from clouds.

SHOWERS
Occasional periods of rain.

SNOW
White frozen crystal flakes of water, falling from clouds.

WIND
Movement of air from one place to another.

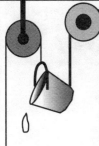

LIGHTNING
A large spark of electricity between clouds and the ground.

THUNDER
A loud "Boom" that follows a lightning.

HAIL
Balls of ice falling from a thunderstorm cloud.

FUNNEL CLOUD: A tornado over land or water that doesn't touch down.
WATER SPOUT: A tornado that touches the water.

TORNADO
A very strong and whirling area of wind that touches the ground.

HURRICANE
A very large and powerful storm, bringing lots of high winds and rain.

HUMIDITY: Amount of moisture or water in the air.
TEMPERATURE: How warm or cold the air is.
PRESSURE: Barometric pressure is the weight of the atmosphere.

CONNECT THE DOG (DOTS!)

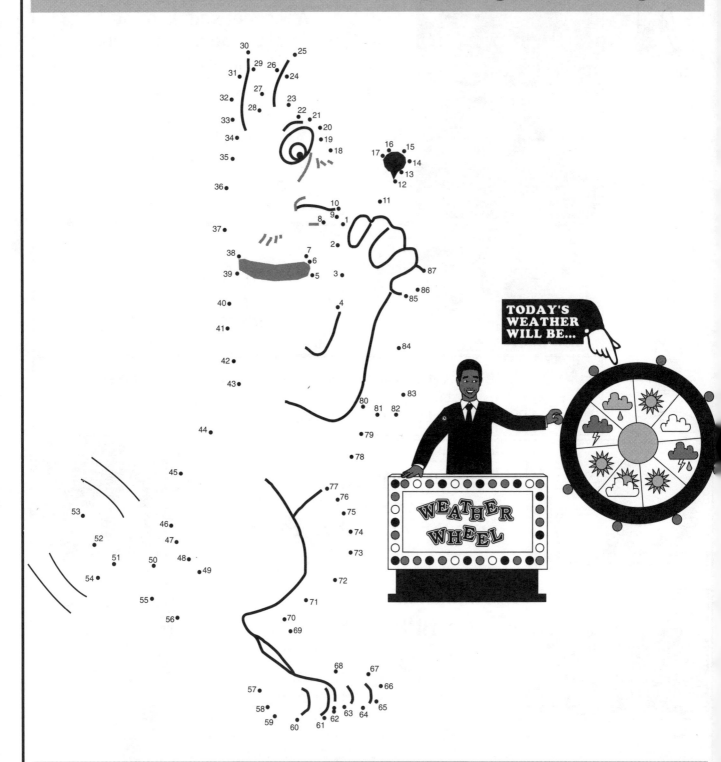

You could Always Pray For Better Weather ! ! !

Tools and Instruments

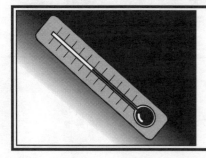

THERMOMETER
This is a tool that measures the amount of heat in the air.

ANEMOMETER
This instrument measures the wind speed, the faster the cups turn, the stronger the wind is.

RADAR
This giant satellite dish receives weather information from all over the world.

AIRPLANE
Airplanes are used to fly under, over and through clouds to measure air pressure and temperature.

SATELLITE
Satellites fly high above the earth in space and send pictures of clouds back to earth for weather forecasters to study.

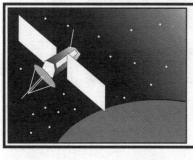

TEMPERATURE

What is Temperature?

Temperature means how warm or cold the weather gets and it all depends on the amount of sunlight.

Imagine a full day, beginning with the time you wake up in the morning to the time you go to bed.

Early in the day, the weather is usually cool. This is because the sun has just risen and has not had a lot of time to shine its warm rays onto the land below. As the day goes on, the sun warms up the earth more and more. The temperature reaches its peak at around 3:00 in the afternoon, and as it begins to set, less energy is received here on the ground and so the weather begins to cool down.

On cloudy days, the daytime temperature doesn't get too warm. This is because the clouds shield us from the sun's warm rays and instead, make for cooler temperatures.

How do we measure heat?

A weather person uses a thermometer to measure how warm the air is. As the temperature rises so does the red liquid in this instrument. There are two kinds of thermometers. Both are the same, but they use different scales of measure. Here in the United States we use the Fahrenheit scale, but in Europe the Centigrade thermometer is very popular. Here is how they're numbered:

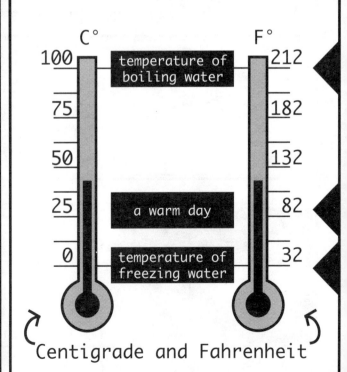

C°		F°
100	temperature of boiling water	212
75		182
50		132
25	a warm day	82
0	temperature of freezing water	32

Centigrade and Fahrenheit

DID YOU KNOW ?

Some people think that you can figure out how warm it is by the number of cricket chirps.

Just count the number of chirps in 14 seconds, add this number to 40, and you get the temperature in Fahrenheit!

Go figure !

EXPERIMENT
Here's What You Need:

1) A half-cup of water

2) A half-cup of soil or sand

3) A thermometer

Place the cups in the refrigerator for 30 minutes then take them out and measure their temperatures at the surface. Write down your measurements in the note pages at the end of this book. Now place the cups in the sunlight for 15 minutes and take their temperatures at the surface. Write down the results. What happened? Although the water and sand both had almost the same temperature after you took them out of the refrigerator, the water has remained relatively cooler than the sand. Why do you think that is? Come up with a few "theories" or reasons why you think the sand gets warmer faster than water; then check your answers with the "answer page" to see how well you did!

CLOUDS

Have you ever looked up at the sky and noticed that not all clouds look the same? In fact no two clouds are identical and they do come in an endless variety of shapes and sizes. However, there are a few distinct kinds of clouds that share the same unique characteristics.

While some clouds only bring us foggy mornings, others bring heavy downpours and lightening, others still just float high in the atmosphere and have no function!

Scientists have classified clouds into three groups. The way they are organized has to do with their appearance and the altitude at which they float.

• Stratus clouds are low clouds that blanket across the sky and turn it gray. They cause fog and at times bring us drizzle.

• Cumulus clouds float higher in the atmosphere. These clouds are responsible for rain and thunderstorms. They look like cotton balls but can stick together to form a big storm.

• Cirrus clouds are very thin clouds that ride very high in the atmosphere. They are so thin that the sun can still shine through them. Often times they warn us about upcoming storms.

DID YOU KNOW?

- It takes the earth one day (24 hours) to make a complete rotation around itself!
- It takes the earth 365 days to travel around the sun. 365 days is one whole year!
- The sun is at the center of our solar system. This puts the sun between 90 million and 93 million miles away from our planet!
- Traveling at about the speed of light, which is 186 thousand miles per second, it takes the sun's energy just over 8 minutes to reach us here on earth.
- The hottest temperature ever recorded on earth was 136° Fahrenheit at the Libyan desert in Libya, Africa.
- almost 75% of the earth's surface is covered by water. Of all that, 99% of it is salty, leaving us with only 1% water to drink, and take showers with!
- You can tell how far away a thunderstorm is by counting! Just count the number of seconds between the time you see the lighting flash and the time you hear the thunder boom. If you counted 5, then the lighting storm is 1 mile away. If you counted 10, then the lighting storm is 2 miles away, and so forth.

BOOM!

HEAT INDEX

Have you ever heard a weather forecaster mention the word "heat index" and had no idea what he or she was talking about? It sounds like it has something to do with heat, but what does the "index" mean?

The amount of moisture, also called humidity, of the air has a lot to do with how warm the air feels. The tiny little water droplets in humid air act like a blanket in keeping your body warmth close to you. As the air gets hotter and humidity increases, the blanket effect gets even stronger! It's almost like wearing a heavy jacket in the hot summer sun!!!

Heat index is also referred to as "how it feels" temperature. This table shows you the warmth you will feel if the temperature and humidity are as follows...

		AIR TEMPERATURE					
		50°F	60°F	70°F	80°F	90°F	100°F	110°F
HUMIDITY	40%	50	60	70	81	93	111	129
	50%	50	60	70	83	96	122	130+
	60%	50	60	70	85	100	129	130+
	70%	50	60	70	88	105	130+	130+
	80%	50	60	70	89	110	130+	130+
	90%	50	60	70	90	126	130+	130+
	100%	50	60	71	91	130	130+	130+

Where Are We?

If you have noticed, a weather person is always standing in front of a map and pointing to different places. So let's see how much you know about the United States and where all the 50 states are. Just match the name of each state with its correct number. Good luck!

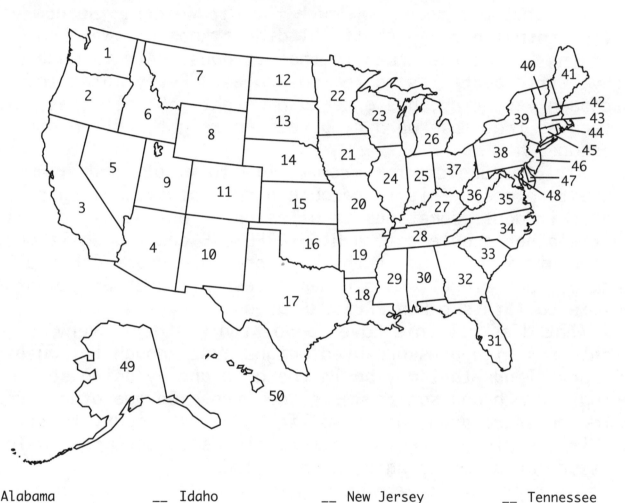

__ Alabama	__ Idaho	__ New Jersey	__ Tennessee
__ Arkansas	__ Kentucky	__ North Dakota	__ Utah
__ Alaska	__ Kansas	__ North Carolina	__ Vermont
__ Arizona	__ Louisiana	__ Nebraska	__ Virginia
__ California	__ Montana	__ Nevada	__ West Virginia
__ Colorado	__ Main	__ New Hampshire	__ Wyoming
__ Connecticut	__ Missouri	__ Ohio	__ Wisconsin
__ Delaware	__ Mississippi	__ Oklahoma	__ Washington
__ Florida	__ Minnesota	__ Oregon	
__ Georgia	__ Michigan	__ Pennsylvania	
__ Hawaii	__ Maryland	__ Rhode Island	
__ Indiana	__ New England	__ South Dakota	
__ Illinois	__ New Mexico	__ South Carolina	
__ Iowa	__ New York	__ Texas	

PRESSURE

What is Air Pressure?

Air pressure means how much the air weighs. So now you may be thinking to yourself, "I didn't know air weighed anything!" But the truth is that it does. Air is made of tiny little particles called molecules. Every molecule, although very tiny, has a certain weight. So all these tiny molecules that make up air, give it a weight, called air pressure.

Air pressure changes from minute to minute and from place to place. This is because air is always moving around, and as it does, sometimes it piles up in one place, creating what weather people call a HIGH PRESSURE areas. While most of the air is tied up in the high pressure area, other places lack air and since less air means less air pressure, weather people call this a LOW PRESSURE areas.

What does all this have to do with weather? Very simple! A high pressure area weighs just enough to squeeze out any clouds that may be in the area and by doing so, brings warmth and sun to where you live. On the other hand, a low pressure area, being so light, needs company to fill all it's empty room. This allows clouds to accompany a low pressure area, bringing rain and clouds.

Air pressure is measured by a barometer. A weather person can easily predict upcoming weather by looking at a barometer. If the air pressure begins to increase, that is a sign of a high pressure and sunny days. If the air pressure decreases, a low pressure must be approaching, bringing clouds and sometimes rain.

PRESSURE

Here, the "high" weight or "high" pressure of the air forces all the clouds away, allowing the warm sun to shine its rays!

cool & dry air

Here, the "low" weight or "low" pressure of the air brings in clouds to make up for it's lack of weight, which brings rain.

Warm air rises and holds up the clouds!

WIND CATEGORIES

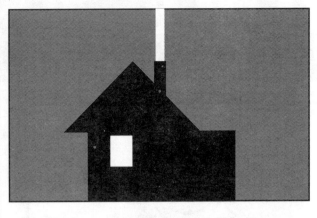

"CALM"

This is when the wind speed is under one mile per hour. Smoke rises straight up. Another name for this wind is the Beaufort category zero (0).

"LIGHT AIR"

The wind speed is between 1 and 3 miles per hour. The Beaufort category is one (1).

"LIGHT BREEZE"

The wind speed here is between 4 and 7 miles per hour. The Beaufort category is two (2).

"GENTLE BREEZE"

The wind speed is between 8 and 12 miles per hour, extending light flags. The Beaufort category is three (3).

WIND CATEGORIES

"MODERATE BREEZE"

Winds between 13 and 18 miles per hour. This is when leaves and dust start to get picked up. The Beaufort scale is four (4).

"FRESH BREEZE"

Small trees begin to sway, when the wind gets up to 24 miles per hour. The Beaufort scale is five (5).

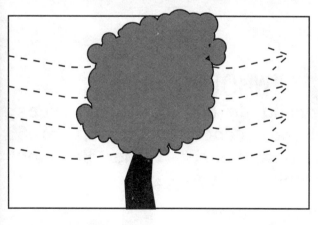

"STRONG BREEZE"

When winds reach the speeds of 25 to 31 miles per hour, it is a Beaufort scale six (6). Big trees begin to sway.

"MODERATE GALE"

Winds between 32 and 38 miles per hour, make it a bit difficult to walk against it. The Beaufort scale is seven (7).

WIND CATEGORIES

"FRESH GALE"
When winds reach the speeds of 39 to 46 miles per hour, and cause small branches to break. The Beaufort scale is eight (8).

"STRONG GALE"
Winds of 47 to 54 miles per hour, which are damaging to homes. The Beaufort scale nine (9).

"WHOLE GALE"
Widespread damage to large trees, when winds reach speeds up to 63 miles per hour. The Beaufort scale here is ten (10).

"STORM"
Winds between 64 and 72 miles per hour, which damage homes. The Beaufort scale is eleven (11).

WIND CATEGORIES

"HURRICANE FORCE"

Oh no! Winds of 73 miles per hour and above will cause destruction. Better hang on to something! On the Beaufort scale, this would be a twelve. (12).

Are you ready to test yourself?

Below, the Beaufort Scale numbers are listed, with a blank space in front. Try to remember what the names of these categories were, and write them in for the appropriate number. P.S. The answer for number 12 is HURRICANE FORCE!

1. _____

2. _____

3. _____

4. _____

5. _____

6. _____

7. _____

8. _____

9. _____

10. _____

11. _____

12. _____

Wind Chill
(Brrrrrr!)

Wind Chill is how cold the air feels, when the wind is blowing. For example, if you blow on the back of your hand, the air hitting your hand feels a little cooler than the room temperature. This is called the wind chill factor. Wind chill factor is usually measured on cold winter days, when the wind is blowing. The chart below shows you exactly how much cooler the temperature feels, when the wind blows at different speeds.

TEMPERATURE

	30°	25°	20°	15°	10°	5°	0°	−5°
10mph	16°	10°	3°	−3°	−9°	−15°	−22°	−27°
15mph	9°	2°	−5°	−11°	−18°	−25°	−31°	−38°
20mph	4°	−3°	−10°	−17°	−24°	−31°	−39°	−46°
25mph	1°	−7°	−15°	−22°	−29°	−36°	−44°	−51°
30mph	−2°	−10°	−18°	−25°	−33°	−41°	−49°	−56°

WIND SPEED

Where Does The Wind Blow?

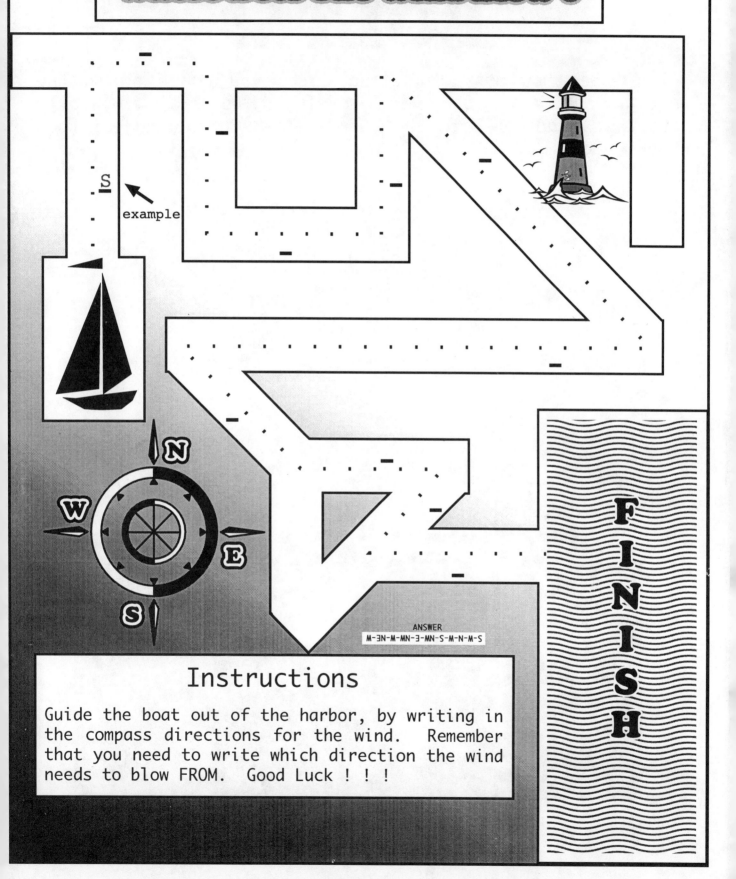

S

example

N

W

E

S

ANSWER
M-ƎN-M-MN-Ǝ-MN-S-M-N-M-S

F
I
N
I
S
H

Instructions

Guide the boat out of the harbor, by writing in the compass directions for the wind. Remember that you need to write which direction the wind needs to blow FROM. Good Luck ! ! !

FIND THE

BOLTS!

See how many lightning bolts you can find in the picture below. Look very carefully to find them all! Check your answer with the answer sheet at the end of this book. Good luck!

It's Prediction Time !

Now that you know about high and low pressures and how they effect the weather, you may be able to predict tomorrow's weather! To do this, watch the weather segment of the news for a couple of days, in the morning and the evening. Write down the barometric pressures in the spaces below for each day along with the high temperatures.

Now look at the numbers carefully. Do you see any patterns? For example, is the barometric pressure getting larger as each day goes by or is it getting smaller?

If the pressure is increasing, that means a high pressure area is building, bringing sunny and fair weather, and if the pressure is decreasing, that means cooler and possibly cloudy weather is in store.

Can you predict tomorrow's weather? How close was your prediction? Write your predictions on the next page and see how close you really came to the actual weather!!

	Barometric Pressure	Temperatures High	Low
Day 1 (Morning)			
Day 1 (Night)			
Day 2 (Morning)			
Day 2 (Night)			

The sky will be _____ (sunny/cloudy/rainy/fair).
The high temperature will be _____ degrees Fahrenheit.
The low temperature will be _____ degrees Fahrenheit.

You should dress accordingly by wearing _____.

Actual weather is:

High temperature: _____°Fahrenheit
Low temperature: _____°Fahrenheit
Conditions: _____

Barometric pressure is only one of the many tools that a weather forecaster uses to predict the weather. To be able to predict the weather more accurately, he or she also looks at pictures of clouds sent from space by one of the weather satellites orbiting the earth.

How would a satellite picture help you in predicting the weather? Explain.

_____

_____

_____

_____

_____

_____

DID YOU KNOW?

- Hawaii is the wettest state! It receives more than 400 inches of rain every year!
- Rain drops are not actually "tear-drop" shaped! Because of the speed at which they fall, their bottoms flatten out so they end up looking like chocolate chips!
- In the Northern Hemisphere, storms and most weather systems travel from west to east! That means that storms bringing rain to us here in California, end up bringing rain or snow or hail to our friends on the east coast a few days later.
- A tornado can have winds up to 350 miles per hour. These winds are so strong that they can actually pick up railroad cars and large trucks and toss them several hundred yards away!
- Lightning is hotter than the sun! The heat from a lightning bolt has been measured at about 50,000° Fahrenheit while the sun's surface is about 11,000° Fahrenheit!
- Outside of Alaska, California's Blue Canyon receives more snow per year (241 inches) than any other place in the United States!
- The highest wind recorded at the Earth's surface was 231 miles per hour atop Mount Washington in New Hampshire.

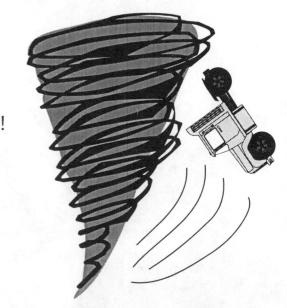

AIR POLLUTION

Have you ever noticed that on some days the sun seems to be shining brighter than others? Or have you noticed that the sky seems blue on some days and brown on others? This brown sky is called air pollution or smog and it happens in most of the big cities around the world.

The reason for this is that factories and cars put out smoke into the air. If on that day there happens to be little or no wind blowing, the smoke and the pollution (smog) don't have anywhere to go and stay where they are, in the sky and right over the city.

This causes the air to turn brown, making it unsafe for people to exercise in or breath for too long of a time. So next time if you hear the weatherman mention that the smog level is "unhealthy", try to keep indoors or try to cut down on running around and exercising, so that you will cut down on the amount of unhealthy air getting into your lungs.

DO NOT BREATHE!!

AIR POLLUTION

   If each and everyone of us puts a little effort into it, we could all help clean up the air in our cities. One easy way that you could help is by walking to school or riding your bicycle, instead of having your parents drive you there. This will cut down on the amount of pollution going into our atmosphere. The same goes for walking to the grocery store instead of driving there, or riding your bicycle to the library instead of being dropped off by your parents.

   Of course there are times that we need to drive to different places such as on rainy days, or when the distance to where you are going to is simply unmanageable and far.

   In these cases, Public Transportation such as city busses, school busses or trains could be a great alternative. Below, list the places you go to every week and ask your parents to measure the distances to those places. See which ones you can walk to instead of having to be driven there. Now you can see how many miles you can subtract from the "Riding" miles and add to the "Walking" miles. Every mile makes a difference, and walking makes for good exercise too. Get your parents involved and see how much fun walking can really be!

Places I Go...	Riding Distance	Walking Distance
	Total:	Total:

Temperature Changes With Elevation (Height) !

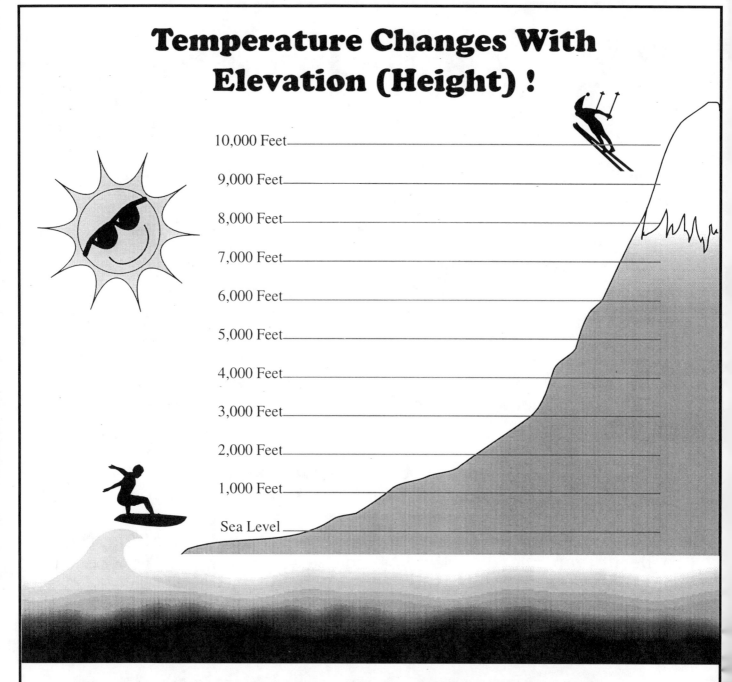

10,000 Feet
9,000 Feet
8,000 Feet
7,000 Feet
6,000 Feet
5,000 Feet
4,000 Feet
3,000 Feet
2,000 Feet
1,000 Feet
Sea Level

Temperature Changes With Elevation!

Have you ever heard the weatherman say that it might snow in the mountains at and above a certain elevation? At the same time, if it is not raining down near the coast, the sun is probably out and the weather is mild. Why do you think that is? Why is it that the mountains usually receive the snow and down near the coast it probably never snows?

The answer is that temperature gets cooler as you go higher up in elevation. It might be warm here at the coast, but at the same time it can be freezing at the elevation of 10,000 feet!

Temperature Changes With Elevation! Continued...

The weather forecasters use a little mathematical equation to find out where the air is cooler and where the snow may fall. This mathematical equation was developed by early weather forecasters and scientists, to better understand and forecast the temperature and weather conditions for any elevation around the world. The scientists came up with a name for this equation:

Lapse Rate

The lapse rate is the rate at which the temperature cools, as you go up in height. So, if you are hiking up a mountain, you will feel that the air is getting cooler as you go higher in elevation. The amount of cooling is about 4° Fahrenheit for every 1000 feet climbed.

This means that if it were 72°f at the beach, at a height of 1000 feet the temperature would be 4°f less than 72°f. So...

$$72° - 4° = 68° \text{ (Temperature at 1000 feet up)}$$

The temperature at 2000 feet would be 4° cooler than that of the temperature at 1000 feet. So,...

$$68° - 4° = 64° \text{ (Temperature at 2000 feet up)}$$

What would the temperature be at...

3000 feet up?
4000 feet up?
5000 feet up?
10,000 feet up?

Now that you know how the temperature drops with height, can you tell at what height snow can fall, if our sea level temperature was 52°f?

ELEVATION EXERCISE...

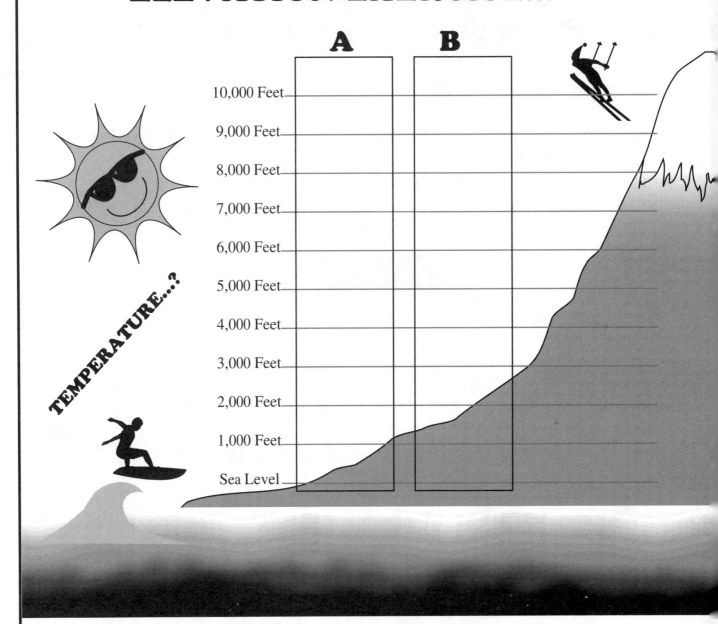

FIGURE OUT THE TEMPERATURE

Now that you know how to figure out the temperature of different places as it relates to height, calculate and write in the temperatures of the different elevations in column "A", if the temperature at 4,000 feet is 71 degrees Fahrenheit.

In column "B" figure out and write in the temperatures of different elevations, if at 10,000 feet the temperature is a cold 25 degrees Fahrenheit.

DID YOU KNOW?

• The water that you drank last night could have been the same water that dinosaurs swam in millions of years ago! How could that be? Well, all the water here on earth is recycled by mother nature. Through a process called the "hydrologic cycle" water on the surface evaporates to form clouds and rain. That means water from millions of years ago has been recycled thousands of times but is still the same water!

• The most rainfall in a short period of time was received in China in 1977. They got 55 inches of rain in only 10 hours!

• Yuma, Arizona is the sunniest place in the United States. They get cloudy skies only 9% of the time during the year. This also makes Yuma the driest region of the United States!

• During the summer months, when the earth (northern hemisphere) is tilted towards the sun, the north pole experiences 24 hours of sunlight for a few months. This means the sun never sets, Zzzz! although it moves down into the horizon a bit!

Seasons

Have you ever wondered what causes the seasons? Why is there a winter, spring, summer and fall?

Our planet Earth not only rotates around itself, creating night and day, but it also revolves around the sun. This process takes about one year or 365 days, during which we experience all four seasons. Because the earth's path around the sun is not a perfect circle, but more like an ellipse, there are times that the earth is farther away from the sun, and there are times that the earth gets closer to the sun.

To understand why seasons occur, we must also remember that the earth is a bit tilted to one side as shown by the illustrations on the next page. All these factors combined gives us the four seasons!

Earth

Sun

Seasons

Why & How...?

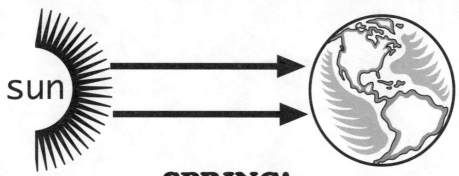

SPRING!

During the spring season, the Earth gets equal amounts of energy from the sun because the Northern and Southern halves of our planet lie equally close to it.

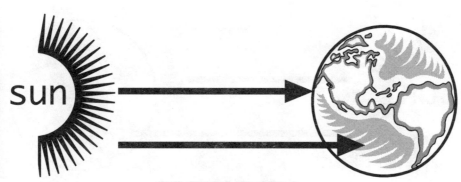

SUMMER!

During the summer months here in the U.S., the Northern half of Earth tilts closer to the sun. This will allow more of the sun's energy to warm us up. Do you know what happens in the Southern half of our planet during this time?

Seasons

Why & How...?

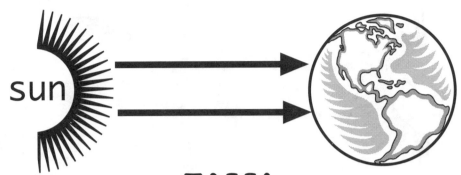

FALL!

During the Autumn, the Earth once again straightens up from the summer tilt, allowing equal amounts of sunshine to reach all of the planet. This means that the temperatures are not too hot or too cold.

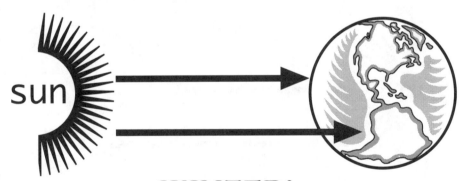

WINTER!

During the winter months here in the U.S., the Northern half of Earth tilts farther away from the sun. The amount of energy coming in to the Northern half of the planet is very little, making it cold and wintry. The Southern half of the planet now enjoys a warm summer!

MISSING SUN!

Start Here!

Find the sun before she sets! Start at the top maze, where it says "Start Here" and make your way down to the bottom where the sun is. Have a friend or parent time you and see how you measure up against the competition!!

My time is: _____

●●●●●●●●●●●●●●●●●●●

4:30-5:00 minutes:
FAIR

3:30-4:30 minutes:
GOOD

2:00-3:30 minutes:
VERY GOOD

1:00-2:00 minutes:
OUTSTANDING
----
under 1:00 minute:
SUPER EXPERT

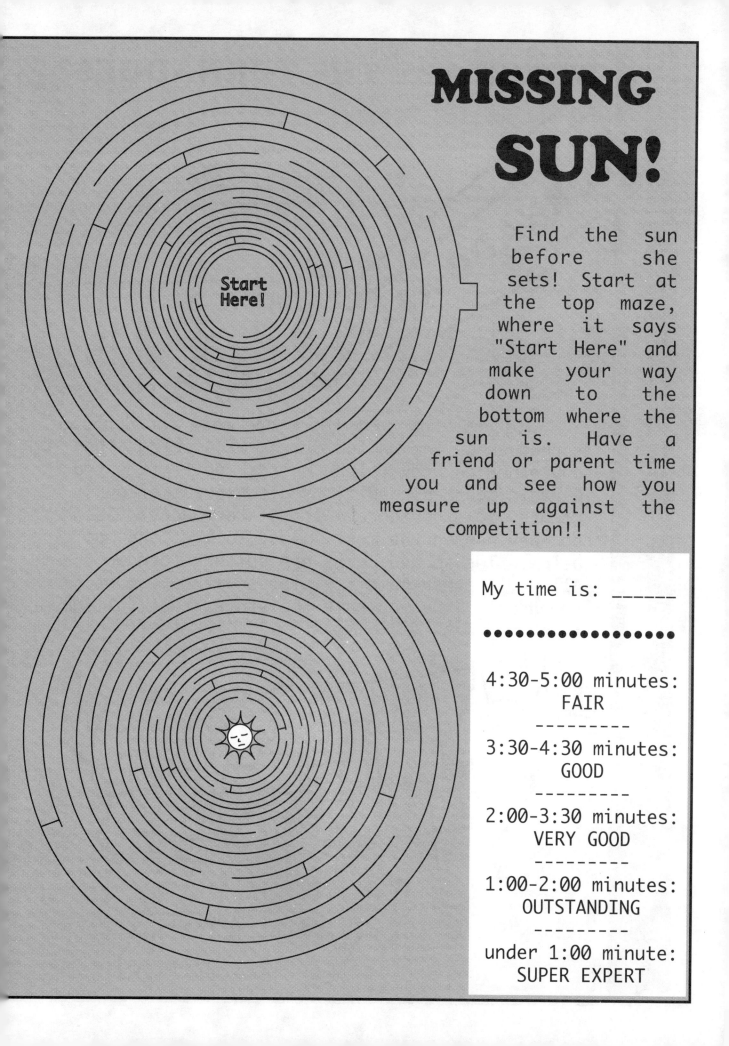

WHERE ARE THE TORNADOES?

Did you know that there are more incidents of tornadoes in the United States of America, than in any other country in the world? Well, it's true! Certain weather conditions allow areas of our country to experience a lot of tornadoes. So where do they happen the most? Just look at the map below. The shaded parts are called "Tornado Alley", another name for places with a lot of tornadoes. Can you name the states that fall under this area?

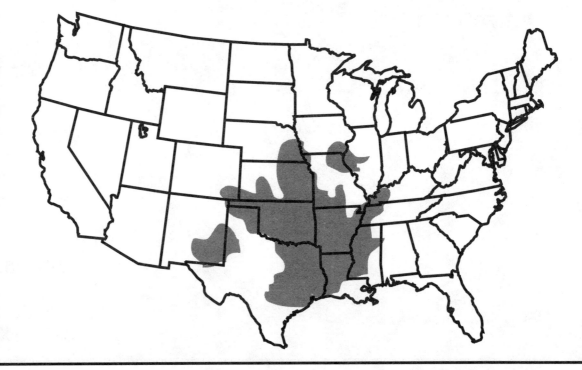

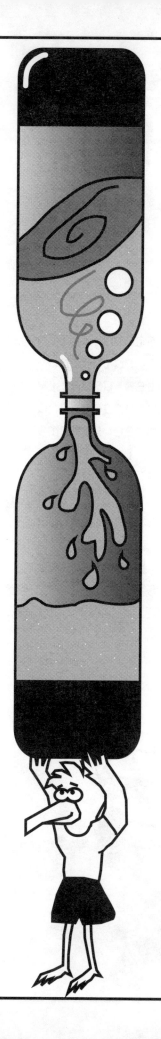

MAKE YOUR OWN
TORNADO
IN A BOTTLE!

Here's What You Need:

1) Two empty 2-liter soft drink bottles

2) Four cups of water

3) Duct tape

4) Food coloring and glitter

To make your tornado in a bottle, pour the water, about one teaspoon of food coloring and a fistful of glitter into one of the empty bottles. Shake well, while covering the top, to mix everything. Next, tape the other empty bottle over the first one using the duct tape. Make sure that you have removed the bottle caps. Also be sure to tape them well enough to avoid any spills! Now comes the fun part! Quickly turn the bottles upside down so that the water pours out from one bottle into the other. As the water pours out, it twirls around making a colorful, glittery tornado in a bottle!

HURRICANE DANGER

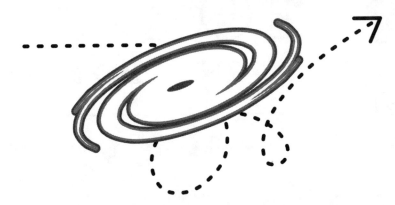

   Hurricane is a name for a very powerful storm, with winds faster than 75 miles per hour, a lot of rain and thunder. Hurricanes that hit the United States usually come from the direction of Africa and grow stronger and stronger over the Atlantic Ocean. Just as these storms reach their most destructive point, they make landfall. The area of the United States that Hurricanes generally hit, is the south eastern section of the country. Although weather forecasters see these powerful storms coming days in advance, they can not yet predict exactly when and where they will make landfall. You could say that hurricanes have a mind of their own! Can you name the states that are effected by hurricanes?

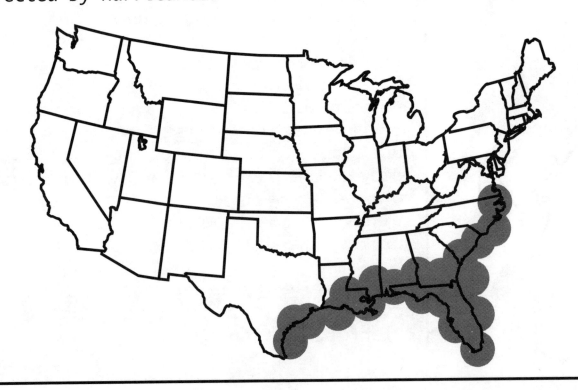

NAME THAT STATE!

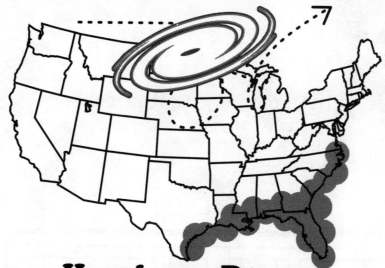

Hurricane Danger

Name the top six "Hurricane" states below:

1 _____   4 _____

2 _____   5 _____

3 _____   6 _____

Where are the Tornadoes?

Name the top six "Tornado Alley" states below:

1 _____   4 _____

2 _____   5 _____

3 _____   6 _____

HERE COMES A TORNADO!

Yikes!

Find your way to the other side of the maze...

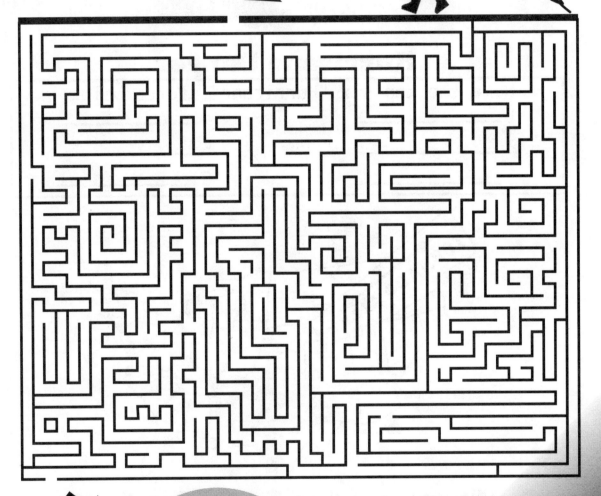

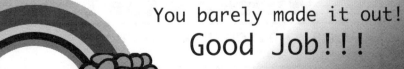

You barely made it out!
Good Job!!!

FIND THE
THERMOMETERS!

There are a few thermometers hidden in the picture below. How many can you find? Check your answer with the answer sheet at the end of this book. Best of luck!!!

HAVE YOU EVER LOOKED
AT A WEATHER MAP, AND WONDERED...

What do those symbols mean on the weather map? Well, if every weather forecaster had to explain everything on a weather map, it would probably take him a good part of the day. And that is only one of the maps. So, weather forecasters came up with little symbols to describe the weather of different regions, without having to verbally explain them. Some of these symbols, such as a drawing of clouds, or the sun or snow are pretty obvious. But on the scientific maps, more important symbols are used to tell the weather forecaster how to forecast the weather! Below, are some of the more basic symbols, along with their description.

 This is called a "COLD FRONT". A cold front tells us that cold air is coming in from the directions from which the arrows are pointing.

 This is called a "WARM FRONT". A warm front tells us that warmer air is coming in to replace the cold air. Instead of arrows, a warm front uses half circles.

 The big "H" stands for "HIGH PRESSURE". This symbol tells the weather forecaster that wherever the "H" is, the weather in that region is fair and sunny.

 The letter "L" means "LOW PRESSURE". This symbol tells the weather forecaster that there will be stormy or cloudy weather in the future.

HELP US SIMPLIFY THE MAP!

Below, you will find a map with explanations written all over it. Your job, is to simplify the map by drawing in the weather symbols you learned on the previous page and the ones you already know. In some cases, you might want to draw in more than one symbol, depending on the weather condition. Good Luck!

Cooling Down

High Pressure & Sunny

Cooling Down & Cloudy

Warming Up

High Pressure & Sunny

Low Pressure & Thunder

Low Pressure & Rainy

Cooling Down

Warming Up

Warming Up & Cloudy (example)

DRAW IN THE FORECAST!

   Sometimes a simple weather map is all you need to see what the weather is going to be like. Below, draw in the weather symbols, using the pictures earlier in the book under the heading of weather terms. Good luck!

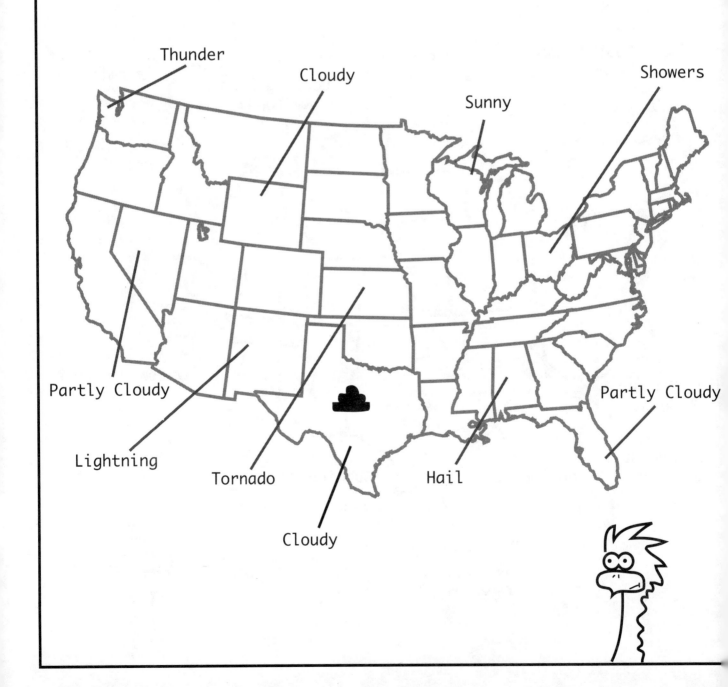

RECYCLE & REUSE

As you know, each and every one of us uses up a certain amount of goods each day. For example, we use water to shower and wash our dishes or we drink milk or soda to quench our thirst. We eat cereal, vegetables, cookies, hamburgers and everything else imaginable to satisfy our hunger.

But what happens to the cereal box that we throw away? Or what about the milk jug or the soda can? The newspaper your mom and dad read, what happens to it? The trash man picks them up and dumps them somewhere else, in a trash dump. But unfortunately the trash dumps are beginning to get fuller and fuller, and the trash keeps on piling up!

That's why each and everyone of us can help reduce the trash by simply recycling. Recycling is when you reuse an item, instead of throwing it away. There are many items that we normally would throw away, which can be recycled.

Items such as soda cans, plastic jugs, glass bottles and newspapers can be taken into special factories and made into clean, new stuff! The soda can you drink out of today, will be made into a brand new can that someone else can drink out of. This way our landfills will not fill up so quickly, and our planet Earth will love us for it!

NEW CANS

OLD CANS

WHAT CAN YOU RECYCLE?

Today there are four major groups of recyclable items such as Glass, which includes glass bottles and jars, Plastic, which includes plastic milk, water or juice containers, Aluminum, which includes aluminum soda cans, and finally Paper.

The other stuff that we throw away such as food particles that include egg shells, fruit skins, leftover meals or anything eatable that finds it's way to the trash, is naturally decomposed. This means that through time, the food rots and it's nutrients return to the soil, helping a young tree or a crop of wheat to better grow in the future.

But as far as those other things that we talked about above, such as plastics, glasses, paper and aluminum, we have to help mother nature, so that we'll all live in a cleaner, better Earth!

So whenever you see the symbol below, think of recycling!

Color in the symbols below, and get your parents to put aside special containers in your kitchen especially for the purpose of recycling. Mother Nature will thank you!

Find It !

There are thirty "weather words" hidden in the puzzle below. Remember, they could be written diagonally, backwards or just the way they should be! Good luck finding them!

```
L I G H T N I N G I M U S R F
T L D U W S L P W D R A E M B
S H O V E R H Q S E F A A R D
E N E A K A A O T I D P S S R
R V W R I N X E W O L F O T O
U R O L M E M M L E C N N Y P
S U N N Y O G A T C R S D O S
S B S L M A M I Z W H U R C U
E H S E N H L E I L O W I D I
R Y N R B L A U T L C L Z A U
P A P U E Z S Z C E Q A Z T R
A N J T H V H E Y V R I L S G
L B A A O M E T E R A R E A T
T S A R D R I K W J D L O C C
I O U E N D N O C B A O K R I
T Q B P I K V A I E R H G E D
U V N M W Q B E D F O G J V E
D T U E P R E S S O L I X O R
E H O T H U N D E R H H W L P
```

Weather Words

Thermometer	Hot	High	Altitude	Lightning
Anemometer	Satellite	Low	Clear	Thunder
Predict	Radar	Cloudy	Overcast	Tornado
Season	Temperature	Fog	Snow	Sunny
Air	Wind	Hazy	Shower	Cold
Humidity	Pressure	Drizzle	Hail	Drops

WHAT IS THE WATER CYCLE?

What is the water cycle? The answer is very simple!
It means the process that recycles water.

Have you ever wondered where the water that you shower
with comes from? Let's follow the path of water as Marty
is getting ready to take his shower. Keep in mind that
water has been on our planet for about 3 billion years.

Of course, rain brings us clean water, which is stored
in dams and water tanks all over the world. But how did
the water make its way up to the clouds in the first place?
The sun's warm energy evaporates the water from oceans and
lakes causing clouds to form, which over time and with the
right conditions bring rain and snow. Most of this rain
water flows back to the oceans and lakes by streams and
rivers. The rest finds its way to water storage tanks
where they are purified and made ready for our use.

When we use the water, it drains into drainage pipes
and eventually gets dumped into the oceans, and as we know,
the sun's energy slowly evaporates this water up into
clouds.

As you see, the water keeps recycling itself with the
help of the sun. That's why it is so important to keep our
waters clean and safe for our use. Although mother nature
does her share of cleaning the water through the water
cycle, we also need to keep our rivers and oceans clean so
we can enjoy clean water for drinking, swimming and taking
baths.

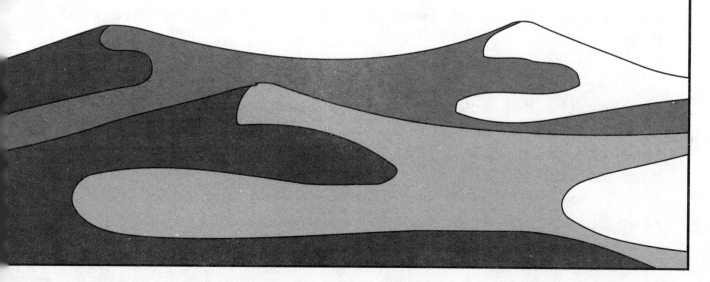

EXPERIMENT

Here is another science experiment you can do

1-Get three clear glasses, all the same size and fill them almost up to the top with clean tap or bottled water.
2-Label the glasses 1,2, and 3 or A, B, and C.
3-Add two tablespoons of dirt to glass 1 or A, then stir.
4-Add two tablespoons of cooking or dark motor oil to glass 2 or B, then stir.
5-Add two tablespoons of water to glass 3 or C and stir.

Which glass would you like to drink from? Most of our drinking water has been on this Earth for about 3 billion years, before man and before dinosaurs. Nature uses the sun and air to evaporate the water into the sky. The evaporating water is pure, not polluted or salty. When the clouds get heavy with this clean evaporated water, the gravity of the spinning Earth helps pull the rain drops out of the sky and down to the ground. There it is collected in rivers, lakes, streams, oceans, and reservoirs where we can use it again and again.

6-Now carefully place the three glasses so that they are exposed to the sunlight, such as behind the window.

Which glass will the sun's energy evaporate first?

7-Mark each glass halfway down with a marker or piece of tape.

Measure each glass on a daily basis. The glass that reaches the halfway mark first, is the winner. You will notice that the one containing only water evaporates faster than the other two. That is because pollutants slow down evaporation and the recycling process.
If we don't keep our lakes, rivers and oceans clean from pollution, then someday we may run out of water!

EXPERIMENT

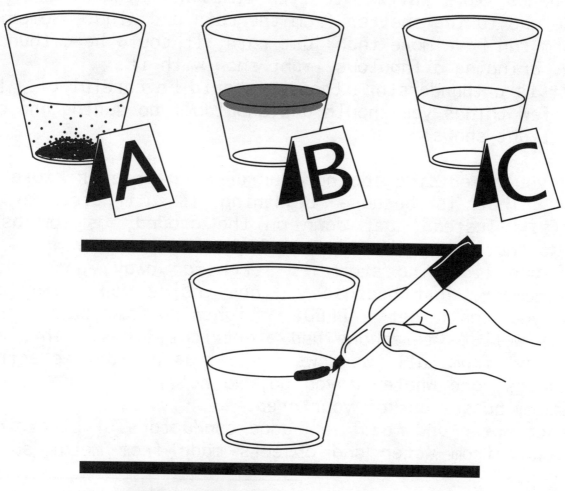

WHAT TO DO IN A STORM!

When a storm rolls in, often times we think of going inside and taking shelter from the rain and wind. Sometimes a storm can have more than just rain, it could be a thunderstorm, bringing a fabulous light show with it.

It is a thunderstorm that we should be careful of. Here are a few things you should and shouldn't do during one of these light shows:

1) If you're outside, do not run under a tree or close to a pole. That is because lightning is attracted to tall objects. Instead, get down on the ground, as low as you can, so that you won't be the tallest object around.

2) If the lightning storm is still far away, get indoors. But remember, just because you are inside your home, don't think you can't get ZAPPED! Lightning can pass through glassas well as telephone and electrical lines. This means get away from all windows, stop using any electrical appliances, and whatever you do, do not use the phone until the storm passes out of your area.

3) Since water and metal are good conductors of electricity, stay away from water and objects made from metal such as door knobs.

WHAT TO DO IN AN EARTHQUAKE?

During a quake, you should duck under a strong table or desk, cover your head and face, and hold onto the table or desk and be ready to move with it. If there aren't any desks or tables around, stand inside a doorway and hold onto the door frame.

- Do not run outdoors.
- Do not run around the house without shoes.
- Get away from large objects that may tip over or fall.
- Beware of your surroundings.
- Try to stay calm.

After the earthquake, make sure everyone is all right and that there aren't any broken objects lying on the floor around you. Calmly join your family and if you have to, evacuate your home using the safest way out. Sometimes being outside isn't as safe as some people think that it is. Power lines, broken glass and falling debris are common dangers during an earthquake. Again, stay calm and watch out for any aftershocks that may occur.

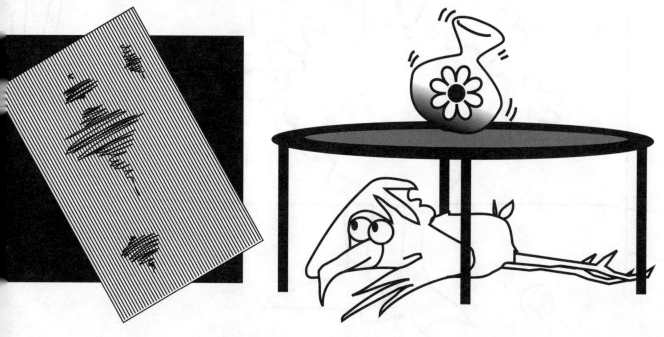

QUIZ TIME

Now you get a chance to see how well you remember the weather terms. Just take a few minutes to match the pictures with the proper terms! Good Luck!

1. Overcast

2. Anemometer

3. Sattelite

4. Lightning

5. Thunder

6. Sunny

7. Oscar the Osterich

QUIZ TIME

When you are done, go back and see if you got all of them right.   If you did, you are one step closer to being a weather person!!!

8. Showers

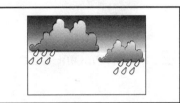

9. Thermometer

10. Hurricane

11. Tornado

12. Christopher

13. Hail

14. Rain

COLOR ME!

NOTES

NOTES

HOW MANY OF MY BOOKS HAVE YOU ALREADY READ?

❏ MUHAMMAD AND THE MARATHON

❏ BEFORE THERE WERE PEOPLE

❏ THE WEATHERMAN IS COMING TO MY SCHOOL TODAY

❏ THE WEATHER PERSON'S HANDBOOK

BOOK ORDERS

To inquire about purchasing this book
or any other books by Christopher Nance
call or write to (818) 831-9268

Christopher Productions, Inc.
10153 1/2 Riverside Drive #266
Toluca Lake, California 91602

We accept Visa, Master Card, or American Express
Please do not send cash.
Make checks payable to: CPI
Returned checks are subject to a service charge for the greater of $15
or maximum allowed by state law.

BOOK SIGNINGS

Please contact us at the above phone number or address if you are having a large book fair
at your school, church, or organization and would like Christopher Nance to attend for a book signing.

FAN CLUB & NEWSLETTER

If you would like to join Christopher Nance's fan club, "The Weatherdude", and be included in our
mailing list to receive a newsletter, send the following information to our office:
Name, Address, Age and Birthday.

Visit us at: www.weatherdude.com

Answer Page

TEMPERATURE EXPERIMENT ANSWER:
HERE IS ONE ANSWER: Darker colors such as soil or sand absorb heat faster; water or light colors tend to reflect sunlight. So the soil or sand when exposed to sunlight should hold the heat and stay warmer. Can you think of another possible answer?

WHERE ARE WE?

30 Alabama	6 Idaho	46 New Jersey
19 Arkansas	27 Kentucky	12 North Dakota
49 Alaska	15 Kansas	34 North Carolina
4 Arizona	18 Louisiana	14 Nebraska
3 California	7 Montana	5 Nevada
11 Colorado	41 Maine	42 New Hampshire
45 Connecticut	20 Missouri	37 Ohio
47 Delaware	29 Mississippi	16 Oklahoma
31 Florida	22 Minnesota	2 Oregon
32 Georgia	26 Michigan	38 Pennsylvania
50 Hawaii	48 Maryland	44 Rhode Island
25 Indiana	43 Massachusetts	13 South Dakota
24 Illinois	10 New Mexico	33 South Carolina
21 Iowa	39 New York	17 Texas
28 Tennessee	40 Vermont	36 West Virginia
9 Utah	35 Virginia	8 Wyoming
		23 Wisconsin
		1 Washington

THERE ARE 9 LIGHTNING BOLTS.

THERE ARE 12 THERMOMETERS.

THE TOP SIX HURRICANE STATES are Florida, Louisiana, Georgia, South Carolina, Mississippi and Alabama. Others include Texas and North Carolina.

THE TOP SIX TORNADO STATES are Oklahoma, Arkansas, Kansas, Texas, Tennessee and Missouri. Others include Mississippi, Louisiana, Iowa and Kentucky.

QUIZ ANSWERS:

 6. Sunny

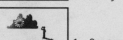 1. Overcast

 4. Lightning

 7. Oscar

 2. Anemometer

 5. Thunder

 3. Satellite

 9. Thermometer

 8. Showers

 12. Christopher

 14. Rain

 11. Tornado

 13. Hail

 10. Hurricane